I0475708

Eight Steps To Publicize Your Company For Free

By Helen Todd, APR

ISBN 978-1-300-659990-7

Eight Easy Steps To Publicize Your Company For Free

Table of Contents

Eight Easy Steps To Publicize Your Company For Free

Introduction

Here you are – an entrepreneur or small business with a great product to sell, and you are not really sure how to go about it.

You don't have a budget to hire a marketing or public relations person, let alone an ad agency. Even if you did hire an agency, how would you determine the value of what you receive?

Whether you think you know public relations and marketing or not, getting your business/product noticed is difficult. Even some of the best PR pros I know have a hard time marketing themselves. It just seems a bit precocious to put yourself out there. But one thing I know for sure: If you don't market yourself, no one else will.

With those thoughts in mind I decided to sit down and put some my collective years of experience down on paper. One thing that I've realized over my 18 years of working in public relations and communications is that regardless of the industry, the approach is universally strategic and most of it is free.

Plan your work and work your plan.

What I do is not brain surgery (if it was, marketing and public relations would require a whole lot more education and training). The following are eight steps you can take to promote yourself without putting yourself out.

Tip: You may not be comfortable doing all eight steps initially. Instead, think about tackling just one at a time. I recommend "baby steps" especially when it comes to the media. A few good experiences will build confidence and lead to the next success.

Advertising vs. Public Relations: I'm not advocating my approach over advertising. Placing ads certainly has its place in a successful strategy. When you are starting out and don't have that kind of money, the following can help get you moving toward your goals. When your business takes off, you may want to explore paid advertising later down the road.

Chapter 1

Step 1: Identify Your Audience

This may seem like a no brainer, but many businesses fail to identify just who exactly they need to talk to. This first step will help you identify who you want to target with your publicity efforts.

It is as easy as writing down who you think will want to buy what you are selling.

1. **Local businesses.**
   - You can find lists of local businesses from your local chamber of commerce, by reading your local business journal or by simply going online and letting your fingers do the walking through your search engine of choice.
   - You can also check in your area for business networking organizations. These are organizations where people usually pay an annual fee, and the people in the group just do business with each other and refer business to each other. In the Birmingham, AL, area there are at least 20 of these different organizations. Once you join one, you can visit the others at no additional charge – that is networking at its best.

2. **Trade associations.** You want to be a member of the trade association related to your industry. **Example:** I am a member of the Public Relations Society of America – at both the national and local chapter. PRSA sets a code of conduct for PR practitioners as well as updates members and educates them on industry trends. It is also the governing board for practitioners who want to earn their accreditation in public relations. These groups also have social media groups to belong to as well.

3. **Media.** These days media encompasses a lot. Print media (newspapers) are online and creating video, radio is online and live streaming, so is television news. Below I explain how to find the appropriate media contacts and how to reach them. The media can help carry the message about your product or service to your target audience. However, reaching out to different media outlets for non-paid or editorial coverage can be tricky. Generally you need to know who you are reaching out to and what topics they cover, and then you have to craft your message. It's a strategic dance of sorts, and I believe it is important to walk through both steps in the process in detail.

4. **Social Media.** Okay – it's not really an audience per se, social media is a tool to reach your audience. It is important though, so Chapter 3 is dedicated to Social Media, the different types and how to manage. Depending on the social media channels you choose, it provides a way to

engage with the audience on an entirely different level. Traditional media outlets carry the message to your audience, but social media engages with your audience, and on a very personal level. Conversely, large companies are getting more detailed feedback on their products by engaging with customers on social media.

5. **Bloggers.** Bloggers belong in a group all by themselves. Some would argue that they belong in media, but they are not necessarily journalists (some are, but some are not). However, bloggers are an important audience. Search online to find bloggers that write about you or your product. Some large technology companies use bloggers to demo software and products before they are released. And, some print media have started following the bloggers. So if a blogger writes a favorable review, it's more likely that the ensuing coverage will be positive as well.

6. **Your employees.** Last, but never least are your employees and/or stakeholders in your company. (Yes, they are internal, but they can also be your best brand advocates as well.) As you try and grow an organization, keep your employees and stakeholders informed on your plans. In fact, if you are going to do these eight free things, I would let them know. They may have contributing ideas.

Is anybody out there?

Now you know who you want to reach, the next step is determining "how" to reach them. We discussed "media" in the list above, the following are some general ideas on seeking out local media channels and specific contact information for reporters. I am assuming that you desire to reach media in a specific city or area. If you want to reach nationwide, then that is a different approach. Whichever approach you take, most media outlets and their contact information can be discovered by online research. I will talk more about "how" to pitch reporters later, but for now, just research and write down your contact names.

Identifying Local Media

Remember, you want editorial coverage in the media....not advertising. Be sure you understand the difference. When you buy an ad, you have control of the content. When you seek editorial coverage, you provide the information for a journalist to package and interpret your content.

1. **Local Business Journal** – Usually a weekly in most communities, the local business journal is an excellent way to reach other businesses in your area. Most reporter names and direct contact information can be found on the journal's website. Seek out a reporter who covers your general area, invite him/her out for coffee, or introduce yourself via email. You want to create a relationship with them of trust where you will provide them timely information and ideas, and hopefully they may write about them.

2. **Business section of your local daily newspaper** – Many daily papers have a business section and local beat reporters (even though the numbers are

dwindling). Monitor your paper for a week and see what reporters appear to be covering your area of expertise. Again, it's up to you to create the relationship and pitch the story idea to the reporter.

3. **Local TV morning shows** – If you are working, you are not sitting home watching television. However, many of your potential clients may be. These days stations are moving toward local programming in the mornings with shows such as "Good Day this...." or "Morning News at...." Each one of these shows has a producer, and that poor producer (I know, I used to be one) has to fill two hours of programming at least every day. It's a grueling job. The trick is to find out who these producers are. Many times their information is not posted online, but a quick phone call to the TV station newsroom will provide the information.

4. **Local talk radio** – Even though many radio stations are now owned by conglomerates, local shows can and do operate independently. And, just like TV, the producers of these radio shows line up guests every day. Who do you listen to? Write it down and look up the station/show to determine the audience demographics. If it matches your audience, write down their contact information.

5. **Community Newspapers** – You may not even know they exist, but if they do, chances are it's the free newspaper sitting in the rack at the convenience store or in your driveway. Even if you don't read it, it's worth checking out because someone does or they wouldn't still be printing it.

6. **Bloggers** – Yes, everyone has a blog these days and if you continue reading, you will too. It is important to identify the bloggers that will potentially review your product or write about your business. The big companies such as Apple and CNN do it. Bloggers are where the online buzz starts, and then reporters covering those industries are also following the bloggers, so they pick up on the story too.

7. **Trade media** – There is probably an online or print media that covers a certain industry such as construction, technology, fishing, or whatever you are interested in. Search online, or at your local bookstore in the magazine racks. You can find contact information for the publication on the inside pages.

8. **Magazines** – They are still a viable medium and getting more localized everyday. Check your local newsstand and seek the publications that are specific to your area and line of business. Buy a copy (they appreciate it) and and note the stories that you liked and who wrote them. On the inside cover or within the first page or two you will also find a page that lists the editorial staff and contributors. You can also search online for a listing, Wikipedia has a list of all U.S. magazines with links to their websites.

Now, you may be asking yourself – isn't it going to cost me a lot of money to get on or in these media outlets above? The answer is no, not if you have a good story to tell. Read on...

Chapter 2

Step 2: What to pitch to the media?

Now that you have identified *who* you want to reach and through what media outlets you can reach them, *how do you pitch your story?*

Your first step in pitching is to determine your approach then pick the appropriate medium.

Like you, the media wants to reach their audience in an entertaining, informative and engaging way. Obviously TV is much different than a print business journal so you need to know what kind of approach is appropriate to pitch to which media outlet. In general the media is looking for stories that follow one of these approaches:

- Is it the first, best or brand new?
- Is it award wining or trend setting?
- Does it solve a problem?
- Does it provide a unique service?
- Is it visual (TV and online mostly, but even print is getting into video)

My recommendation is to figure out what you have to pitch, and then pick the appropriate medium.

When you don't have a new product or something visual that someone can come take a picture of, you might focus on selling yourself to the media as an expert. If you can identify a trend or something in the media that you can provide meaningful commentary on, then offer yourself to reporters to provide commentary.

- For example, say Trinity company has just released the latest smart phone with a GPS dog locator. Your pitch will not only provide commentary on why that is groundbreaking (finding lost dogs), but also what some of the drawbacks may be for the public (such as short battery life or low data storage). By positioning yourself as an expert, your company name makes it into editorial coverage all while positioning you as a go-to person in the community. I talk more about how to become an expert in Chapter 6.

How to Approach the Media

Now you know what you want to pitch, but how do you do it? Start with a News Release, Email pitch, or Photo Opportunity. Depending on what information you want to convey, you will want to consider these different approaches. Each has its place, but with the strength of web, I'm seeing fewer formal press releases and more informational e-mail pitches.

Variations on the Traditional News Release

First I'm going give you some alternatives and then give you a template for doing a press release. That's right – the new reality is that reporters, regardless of the medium are even more strapped for time and resources than ever before. If you write a news release you have two sentences to get your point across before you loose them, and one of those is the subject line. I recommend a format as simple as the one below:

This format works especially well for events or photo opportunities – when you have something visual you want

Headline

Who:

What:

When/Where:

Why:

Contact:

the media to cover., This is a "Just the Facts" way of getting the information delivered in a clear, concise manner. I've used this approach in every line of business I've worked in, from non-profit to healthcare. It works every time – if the information is truly newsworthy.

Let's walk through an example of how to put this together:

Headline:

Steel Company Demonstrates Strength of New Building Material

10 a.m. Wednesday, April 21st at Fair Grounds

[You want to make sure that you put the Who, What, When and Where in the headline]

Who: Joe Steel Company, creator of titanium rods, will demonstrate the strength of a new material for the building industry. The material will help homes and businesses survive dangerous outbreaks in severe weather. [This is where you may elaborate. For example if a certain someone from the company will be speaking, showing or partnering...you may tell more about it here, but still keep it brief.]

What: The company will show how new the material stands up in severe situations by having a truck run into the materials at 70 mph, the strength of a tornado winds. [The "what" can be anything, but if you want the media to come to you, it needs to be visual. You may have worked with a family or business to solve a problem, have them there to help you tell the story – its doesn't have to be this dramatic.]

When/Where: Fair Grounds, located at [insert address with zip code for gps users. If there are any particulars on parking or where to go, give it here.]

Why: Joe Steel Company believes that no family or business should have to experience the horrific damage of a tornado. That is why we have worked for 10 years on developing and testing this new product. [This is where you can talk more about your company and your passion for your product and why it solves a problem for your audience.]

Contact: Helen Todd at helentodd35@gmail.com or call [insert number].

> **Tip:** Whomever you put as the contact needs to be available to answer questions. You can't put contact information here and then not respond. And, you have to respond quickly. The media wants things when and where they want it, and if they are offering coverage you must be accommodating.

Email Pitch

So the above is one method for putting your information together, but maybe you don't have a strong visual, maybe you are more of an expert in a certain area and can provide guidance or commentary on an issue. Maybe there is not a who, what, when and a where – there is just you. You can pitch yourself via an email pitch. Again, you still only have a couple of sentences to grab the attention of the reporter, so make it count – but don't over exaggerate. Reporters hate it when you overpromise and under-deliver.

Subject: Joe Steel Company has tips on how homeowners can rebuild stronger

[insert reporter name],

I noticed last week that you wrote about "x" – I'm the owner of company "y". As a company working in the industry we have noticed the trend of "w". We believe we have a new way of building homes and businesses that will help save them in future storms. We welcome the opportunity to discuss this new method with you and your viewers. My contact information is below, let me know if you are interested.

The Full Monty News Release

If you feel that you have more detailed information to offer than either of the above methods you will want to use a full-scale news release. It can also serve as the back up to both of the above methods. Say, for example, you do a photo op to get media to your event. At the event you can hand out the full news release. I would also use a news release if you are going to make an official announcement for your company or organization. It is a formal statement of an organizations actions, and when posted online on a company's website, it can serve as a company's archive of publicly stated information. Publicly traded companies use news releases to formally state earnings as well as other matters they want noted for public record. But, they can serve less formal purposes as well. Over time, a well-kept archive of news releases gives reporters interested in your company a road map of your organization. The following is a template for a news release.

[insert company logo]

For immediate release
[insert month, day, year]
Media Contact: [name]

JOE STEEL COMPANY ANNOUNCES NEW PRODUCT TO HELP HOMES AND BUSINESSES REBUILD STRONGER TO WITHSTAND FUTURE TORNADOES

Birmingham, AL – Joe Steel Company announced today that it has developed a patented new material to make future homes and businesses withstand tornadoes with winds up to 70 mph. The new material was unveiled at a demonstration at the Fairgrounds.

"Our company has been working for ten years on this new product and today was an historic announcement not just for us, but for the entire community that has suffered reoccurring damage from tornadoes," said Joe Steel, president and CEO of Joe Steel Company. "This is just the beginning for us. We plan to partner with builders across the region to help incorporate this material in all new structures, making people feel more safe."

About Joe Steel Company

Joe Steel Company formed in 1996 as a materials manufacturer of composite boards. The company is a leader in green manufacturing and building projects. Joe Steel Company is located in [insert city, state] and is dedicated to improving building products for the future. We can be found on the web at [insert web address].

###

Let's dissect the news release sample and get it into some meaningful chunks so that you can apply it to anything.

Headers: The top is basic and should be standard each time. Your company logo, the date the news release is going out, "For Immediate Release," date, and contact information. These are the standards each time. Put the headline in all caps, bold it and center it. I usually make it in 14-point typeface and the rest of the release in 12 point - not bold.

The News Release: Use Associated Press (AP) style. It begins with the city and state. If you are not familiar with AP style guidelines I encourage you to learn to use them. In short, it is the set of style guidelines for the print media to write news stories, and therefore it's the language of reporters, which increases your chances of coverage. However, with newspaper numbers dwindling, fewer media actually strictly adhere to AP guidelines. I still use it, so it may be the reason you wonder why I didn't capitalize the CEO's title. That is an AP style rule. I'm old school when it comes to style – it's just how I roll.

Lead paragraph: Make sure you use inverted pyramid style putting the most important information in the first paragraph. I like to follow it with a quote from whomever is appropriate. Quotes are rarely used verbatim, but sometimes, if a reporter can't make it to the event, they have the option of using these quotes. Every news release should also answer the basic journalistic questions of who, what, when, where and why. If it doesn't answer these questions then be prepared for the media to ask them.

Close: At the bottom you will notice I have the "About the company" paragraph. This is called a "boilerplate." This is your standard paragraph about your company that says who you are and what you do. It should be on everything and is a part of "branding" your company. This helps tell the media a little bit more about you, any relevant facts about the size and scope of your organization and where they can get more information.

> **Tip:** Make news releases meaty. Try to anticipate the questions media might ask such as, how much will it cost? What are the regulatory concerns? How was the item tested? If you are not comfortable sharing the details and answering the hard questions – then you shouldn't be soliciting media coverage.

Wire and other Distribution Services

You may have heard some people talk about "wire" or online distribution services. I wanted to take a moment to explain what these are and why you may or may not want to consider using one.

The Associated Press wire distribution service basically puts third party content into the hands of media subscribers. It is a non-profit organization. Basically, this service charges by the word to distribute your information.

It is distributed to all media in a specified state or region, which subscribe to it. You can also request national or international distribution.

Services such as PR Newswire, Business Wire and Market Wire also facilitate getting your news release on the wire, but for usually for a fee. I'm not knocking these services, in fact I have used them when I worked at publicly traded companies that required certain disclosure requirements or with a client that is looking for regional or national coverage But in reality, unless you are trying to reach an entire region of the country, or a national audience,, by doing the media research we discussed in the beginning you can formulate your own media list for free, and distribute your news release for free. Plus, the media appreciates it when someone reaches out to them directly instead of expecting them to pick something up off the wire.

Chapter 3

Step 3: Social Media

While, you may be familiar with social media and how it works, I'm assuming you don't know how to use it for your business. The following explanations/definitions help you begin.

I don't claim to be an "expert" in social media, but I've been around it enough to know that it can be used to great success – and great detriment.

This is a high level overview, and I define only a few social media tools below. There are many, many more. My recommendation is to pick one or two social media outlets that fit your business and explore those. It is possible to eat up all of your time and energy on social media alone.

The goal in using social media for business is to engage with customers. Be a part of the discussion on your industry or specialty and gain a share of the online audience

In all of these mediums don't be afraid to "friend" or "follow" reporters that you like and who may cover you. Your ideas or posts may spark story ideas for them.

LinkedIn – This professional social media tool allows you to identify your credentials and network with professionals in and outside your immediate circle. It is important to update your profile on a regular basis, check for messages and screen people who are asking to link to you. As frustrating as it may be, there is spamming and some will just try to link to you, to sell to you. LinkedIn is a great way to find and belong to professional groups. It is also a great way to get references on the work you do.

Facebook – This casual social media tool has launched brand pages for businesses. Also, where you once thought that all posts were public, now in the new timeline format (Spring 2012) you can group friends in tiers of family, close friends, friends and public. That way you can target posts just for those groups, limiting who will see them. Brand pages are a great way for a company seeking to interact with a broad audience to receive feedback, which is crucial to marketing to a mass audience. Consider this, according to Facebook, more than 845 million monthly active users used the site at the end of December 2011. That is a lot of potential buyers. Facebook plans for users to stay online, and do all of their browsing and communicating in that one medium. On the converse side, younger demographics say that Facebook is less important. I'm not sure I'm buying that, but with it's public stock offering controversy it does appear to have its issues. Issues aside….845 million people isn't something to dismiss lightly.

Google+ -- Just launched in the fall of 2011, this is Google's social media answer to Facebook. While it lacks the numbers of Facebook, it is growing in popularity. With attractive features such as creating circles of friends, you can group people according to audience. However, Google+ limits how large circles can be, and you must manually maintain them (at least at the time of this writing). The cool thing is you can do video "hangouts" in Google+, which is proving popular. Again, there are very practical uses for this tool, but it does depend on your business and whom you are trying to reach.

Pinterest – This social media pin board allows Facebook and Twitter users to "pin" images of interest. This might be useful to a company trying to brand themselves to a larger audience, such as a book, photos, recipes, software for home-users. It is a great way to have people "recommend" your product or service. It's posts tend to be aspirational, so if you have a product that consumers aspire to, this may work for you. It was launched in the fall of 2010 and is one of the fastest growing social tools.

Twitter – You've probably heard of it, but this social medium allows users to share thoughts, photos or commentary in an entry of 140 characters or less. If you want to position yourself as an expert in an industry or topic, this is a great way to get out there. Probably one of the biggest questions is how much to "tweet" or post your comments. Some people tweet several times a day, while others only when they feel necessary. I prefer not to tweet every thought, emotion or lunch – but rather to share a thoughts on a local news item or to ask a question. It does take a while to build a following and tweeting does require consistency. You also build a following by following others. It's pretty simple actually.

Foursquare – Basically lets people "check-jn" at a restaurant or other type of location on a map and rate/talk about their experience. It connects in with Facebook and Twitter. If you are a retail location – food or otherwise, being on Foursquare makes sense.

So you are probably asking if these social media outlets take up too much time to track success. Several social media tools help manage posts. Check out Postling, Tweetdeck, HootSuite, and Dlvr.it.

Postling used to have a free option but now charges a minimum of $5 a month, but the service it provides in terms of tracking and posting is very good. Hootsuite does still have a free option, but of course for $5.99 a month you receive a few more bells and whistles in terms of analytics and opting out of ads that may be worth the price. Dlvr.it, is also good, offering basic free services and premium for businesses.

As with anything, start small/free to see what really meets your needs. Before you stick your toe in the social media water, you may want to gather an outline of what you want to say. Many companies develop a social media editorial calendar of sorts, a schedule that maps out each week's actions and goals.

The social media management tools I mentioned above allow you to schedule posts, which is good when it comes to business, but remember half of the reason people want to engage with you is because they are interested in your personality and what you have to say. Don't be afraid to be spontaneous.

Caution: Remember that spontaneous is not stupid.

Things you should never post:

- Bad meeting with client
- If you are feeling sick. Please don't give details
- Politics – you can't win. It doesn't matter what side you are on [of course if your company is lobbying for certain legislation like high gravity beer, you may want to plead your case.]
- Pictures of you in a hot tub

Anyway, you get the drift. My mom is now on Facebook, so I try to remember if I post it – my mom is going to see this. Not a bad rule of thumb.

Chapter 4

Step 4 – Free Directory Listings

In additional to social media, you also need to claim your business in online directories such as Google Places, Yelp and Yahoo. You can also obtain free listings in directories such as Yellow Pages online. Both offer paid and non-paid listings,. Always opt for the free ones.

Claiming your business in these sites lets you know and respond when people have something nice or something bad to say. If someone has something bad to say online, take the conversation off-line. However, unless your business deals with the public en-masse, you won't have many issues here. If you do, the following are a couple of scenarios and ways to respond.

> **Post:** I was very unsatisfied with your product it did not do what you promised.

> **Response:** Thanks for bringing this to our attention, if you will contact us at [insert number] we would be happy to talk through the issues you had with the product. We want to make sure our customers are happy.

> **Post:** I have already contacted you and your receptionist was rude.

> **Response:** Wow, that is truly not how we do business. Please contact me directly at [insert email

address] I would like to talk through the experience with you.

Post: You have already refunded my money, I don't want to talk with anyone, I just want to complain.

Response: Well, it is certainly your right to post here that you are not happy, but I want others who see this to know that we value all of our customers and want to do everything possible to meet their needs.

If the person continues to post I would not engage in a back-and-forth exchange more than this. I would also reach out to happy customers and ask them to post about their experience. It will push down the negative ones. Remember, responding to negative posts is like responding to a frustrating email. Just count to 10 or get up and walk away. Social Media is not the place to engage in a debate. There have also been recent news headlines where "hackers" have gone online and posted bad reviews, etc. for a restaurant, trying to solicit a gift certificate or refund, a type of online blackmail. This is the lowest of the low. I saw where one business owner took his fight to the media and got coverage for fighting back against the online blackmailers.

Chapter 5

Step 5 – Your website

For the purposes of this book, I'm assuming that you already have a website for your company. The following are suggestions on how to make sure that site is working for you.

It is easy today for people to craft their own websites, and there is certainly nothing wrong with that, but don't get carried away with the bells and whistles.

There have also been changes in the way search engines function. You want to make sure your content is dynamic, and tagged appropriately to help your site pops up in "organic" searches in search engines such as Google and Yahoo. Organic search means a web site comes up because of key word relevance--not paid advertising.

Essential elements of business websites:

- Company Overview – what does your company do?
- Who runs your company – brief pictures with bio (with some personality)
- Short 2-3 minute video about you or your company (hosted by YouTube)
- Photos –, especially if you are selling a product
- A contact us page – to provide a general way for people to get in touch with your company. Be

sure to include a form that captures contact information from those interested.

- Success stories – These can be written by you or by your customers.
- Rich Content -- both images and pages, are properly "tagged" and have the right "meta data" for Search Engine Optimization (SEO) purposes.

Essential Elements to leave out:

- A company overview that overruns page and is more than two to three sentences.
- A video so long or boring that no one would watch it
- Images so large that delay downloading
- An annoying opening page that people have to wait through to access the essential information. You may want your page to fashion an "experience" but viewers rarely have time for it.
- Contact information form that isn't monitored. Make sure you answer queries or designate someone in your organization to respond immediately. They can politely weed the legitimate requests from the spam.

Search Engine Optimization (SEO)

SEO is an important component for websites, especially those that don't want to pay to rank in search engine rankings. Your page should appear when people are looking for you organically. While there is nothing wrong for paying for search rankings – my book is about "free" stuff you can focus on. There are companies who focus on nothing but SEO. . I'm sure there are SEO experts out there who would have a lot to add to this section. The following is an overview.

SEO is the process of writing, tagging and entering the right metadata for your web pages with the proper terms. Regardless of how your site is configured in order for you to get picked up organically in web browsers you need to have the right combination of content and "tags." Tags are the few key words that describe your content. The below is an example from my kayaking blog. I have tagged the post with the keywords: Little River Canyon, Chairlift, Bottleneck. I could also have added kayaking and whitewater..

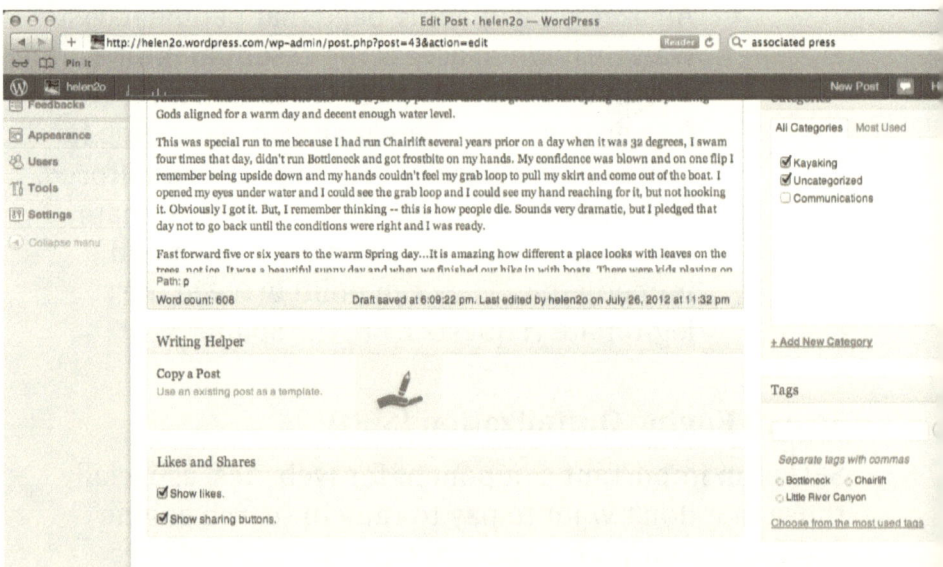

It is also important to tag images and video on your page that when you upload them with similar key words.

Metadata is similar, but it is usually a phrase that is entered just like a tag that describes what the page is about. It is important to use the same key words that you have used in the tags. And don't forget to include location. An example of a metadata provided for the above-mentioned page would be: Whitewater kayaking on the Little River Canyon in northeast Alabama.

Another way to keep your website appearing higher in search engine rankings is to keep the content fresh. Have a blog or post an event your group is having or attending -- add something new at least twice a month, once a week if possible. The blog idea I will talk about in the chapter on becoming an expert.

Another free thing you can do for your website is to link to other sites. Link to industry trade associations, link to other people you do business with, and more important ask them to link back. You also want to cross-link the pages in your site. For instance your front page should link to your contact page and your contacts page should link to your leadership page and so on. Linking is another great way to improve your search engine results. External links that link back to you bring in traffic from other sources and the internal links keep your visitors on your page longer.

Chapter 6

Step 6 – Become an Expert—So Start a Blog

This paragraph should be titled, "realize you already are an expert." Let's face it. If you are entrepreneur, no matter what the product, you are an expert on that product and in your industry. For example, maybe you developed a new pipe fitting for pumps. You are an expert on irrigation. You can create a blog and talk about the process that led to the creation of the new product. Why is it better than others? What benefit does it bring to the industry as a whole?

Remember when we talked about what makes something worthy of news coverage? Those are the same things that make you an expert. Create a blog and talk about it. Talk about industry trends and where you feel things are headed. Find an article you like and post about it and link to it.

A blog can also form the basis for your social media posts. Write the blog, then pull from the blog and make them your posts. Using one of the social media management tools I suggested in Chapter 3, you can also schedule them. And, if you've "linked to" and/or are "followed" by reporters – this gets your information in front of them. Blogs don't have to be super lengthy. Posts around 200 words are good, and you can make them visual by adding photos. In fact that makes them better and more engaging. I use WordPress to set up my blogs and it was super easy. I equate it to the Geiko commercial – so easy a caveman [women in my case] could do it.

Not comfortable writing? Well hire someone like myself to do it for you, but it really isn't that difficult. Some of my tips for writing and proofing are as follows:

- When you have the thought, just sit down and write it out – no matter where you are. If you write the idea down you can come back to it later and flesh it out.
- Having problems writing? Then sketch out an outline. Sometimes I just write down bullet points like this. Later you can go back and fill them in.
- Once I write something, I usually leave it for 24 hours before reading it again.
- Read what you have written out loud. Okay, people around your business or family may look at you strange, but I've never gotten complaints from my dogs. When I worked in an office I would close the door. This method really helps catch mistakes.
- Read what you have written backwards, from the last sentence to the first. It makes your brain focus on how you're writing rather than what you're writing.

Chapter 7

Step 7 – Get Involved

It is important for any business owner to be involved in the community. Look for groups and associations that align with your priorities.

Non-profits enable you to meet others in the community. While you can't call up an acquaintance and ask 'hey can I be on your board,' you could call and say 'hey, I have this product and I think you guys might appreciate it and because you are a non-profit I'll let you have it for free if you wouldn't mind recommending it to others if you like it.' You can also simply volunteer for an organization you are passionate about and get to know the people in and around the organization.

Entrepreneur groups, trade associations and Rotary clubs are also excellent networking sources to help grow your business. While Rotary club membership is not free, you can usually visit for at least one or two times to determine whether the membership is a good fit for you (and worth the expense).

Or, ask if these groups are interested in having you as a speaker.

Don't forget your local Chamber of Commerce. While this membership may entail a fee, look for membership options that put you and your product in front of others.

Once you become a member, take advantage of the networking – after hours mixers, breakfast meetings with community leaders, workshops to help small business, promotion on their website. While you may not be the most outgoing person personally, a couple of hours of meeting new people will expand the chances of adding to your businesses success.

Chapter 8

Step 8: Consistently Brand Your Business

Chances are your company already has a logo and a name. If not, it is something to think about. Your company name and logo should be something you use on everything: business cards, email signature, company letterhead (even if electronic), advertising, signage.

Your name and logo are the image that says who you are and what you do. Many companies develop a logo and what they call a "tag line," which is just a few short descriptive words that provide clarity about your business. The following are just a couple of examples of well-recognized logos and tag lines:

- Allstate – You're in Good Hands
- Alabama Power – Always On
- Alagasco – We're the Good Heat
- American Express – Don't Leave Home Without It
- MasterCard – Master the Possibilities

You get the drift. It is important not to make logos and tag lines too lengthy. If you have a complicated brand or service it may be worth your time to invest in a marketing person or agency to help you develop that brand. Let's assume you already have one. The following are some ways to leverage it.

Remember when we talked about the free online listings in Chapter 4? Make sure your company and brand are listed here. Create brand pages on social media sites such as Facebook, FourSquare, LinkedIn and Google+. Engage with your audience by asking questions and holding a contest. Thinking about making an improvement to your product? Ask your followers and friends to give you feedback. It is a great way to do informal research.

If your company participates in an annual industry or trade association meeting, think of an inexpensive gift to take with you with your logo on and contact information on it. Companies sell products for around a $1 that make great giveaways. Ideas include stress balls, hand sanitizers, detergent pens, fans, key chains, water bottles – look online and don't be afraid to be creative. One of my favorite giveaways at a healthcare trade show was a globby ball. I would toss it against a wall and it would stick, then slowly release then fall to the ground --tons of goofy fun. Everybody else thought so as well.

Consider sponsorships, such as your son's little league team or a golf hole at a charity tournament, to brand your company. Make sure to supply your logo to emblazon t-shirts, sponsor lists and everything else associated with the event.

You also want to be careful with the usage of your logo. When I worked at *Southern Living* magazine we were conservative about our logo. We didn't give it to anyone unless we were assured we would have prior approval of all usage. To this day I'm a logo hound. Even the well-intentioned can distort or change the color of a logo, making it look ridiculous. In addition to getting your logo out there, protect your branding. Just a word of caution.

Bonus Chapter 9

Tips for Working with the Media

We talked in Chapters 1 and 2 about how to identify the media and what to send to them, but the following are some do's and don'ts for talking to them and developing a good working relationship.

Do – read your local papers or search the internet and find reporters who cover your area.

Don't – mass email reporters hoping to snag the right one.

Do – send an email to a reporter offering your story idea.

Don't – keep asking them if they are going to do the story. If you've sent the pitch once and they acknowledged it, then move on.

Do –ask a reporter to have coffee or lunch.

Don't – call when they are on deadline. If they don't want you to pick up the check, let them pay for their own lunch. Some reporters have very strict guidelines even today on the appearance of someone trying to buy their favor.

Do - call the assignment editor at a TV station and follow up to ask if they received your information.

Don't – ask them if they are going to be at your event. Most of the time they will not know until the last minute.

Do – pitch the media on your news conference or event

Don't – over sell it. If you promise monkeys riding dogs like at the local fair – you better have it.

Do – call a reporter and tell them you liked the story they did.

Don't – call and tell them you hated it. Unless a reporter got something factually incorrect don't call and tell them you were disappointed with a story because it didn't turn out as big or with the headline you wanted. Sometimes a story being cut or edited is out of reporters' control. You can end up just rubbing salt in the wound.

Do – call and ask a reporter if you can review your quote for a story

Don't – expect to review the entire story before it runs. I have only known one or two magazines that would actually allow a company to review a story before it went to print. Print journalists almost always strictly adhere to not letting a person review their story.

Timing

Timing is everything. I didn't coin the phrase, but it's true. Timing is crucial in reaching out to the media as well as using social media.

Each medium--print, TV and radio—has its own cycles. All are on 24-hour news cycle. I know first hand. Back when CNN started "24 Hours News" back in the 90's I became the 24-hour news part of the local then ABC affiliate, now turned Fox affiliate. After three and half years of hard work I had been promoted to the producer of the "Daybreak" show. That meant I worked overnights, going in at 10 p.m. and leaving the office at 8 a.m. While I wrote the one-hour news show, I would have to stop twice an hour, run over and sit in front of a live static camera and do a live news cut-in. My mother thought I had reached the pinnacle and was a star. (Nobody loves you like your Mom.) My friends who sat in the bar and watched, called me "Helen in a box." The point is, the news business is always about what is breaking. You can plan to have the biggest, greatest event in the entire world, but if a bus full of nuns carrying babies runs off a cliff, the news will focus on that.

There are also times of the day when it is more convenient for news sources to cover something. Below is an outline of different mediums and when is a good time to contact them.

Radio – Pretty much anytime with a live show. Radio can tape segments, but having someone on live is preferable. Radio stations also offer taped weekend public affair shows. If you are involved in a charitable event or something as a public service, this may be of interest to them. Contact: the news director or news reporter.

TV – Most TV stations reporters come in at 8 a.m. They meet at approximately 9 a.m. to see what they are going to cover that day. They meet again in the late afternoon to see what they are going to cover that night. They decide where to send to reporters and photographers based on these meetings. Your event needs to be in the assignment editors cue before these meetings to be considered – that is unless you are breaking news. Most companies don't want to be breaking news – it usually isn't positive. Contact: Assignment editor, producer or reporter.

Print – daily vs. weekly – You wouldn't think that these two mediums would compete but they do (now more than ever since the industry is tight). For papers large enough to have a business section, find out what day of the week they put out their section and what the deadline is. Daily business news sections can get coverage for new products, entrepreneur ventures, business event listings and new hire news. Weekly business papers are a bit different. You need to find out what day they publish. The deadline is usually the afternoon before to make the print edition. Contact: reporters that cover your beat.

Bloggers/Online – Every one of the mediums listed above does online. I suggest trying to develop a relationship with a reporter or blogger that may cover you consistently.

You do not want to have your event in the middle of another crisis. You are probably asking yourself – how will I know? The answer is you won't. If severe weather hits – postpone your event. If a major building is on fire downtown – don't call the TV station and ask them if they are going to be at your grand opening. If you are having a news conference or open house and there is a shooting somewhere else, chances are that is what they are going to cover.

You also need to know when to call the media to follow-up and make your pitch. The following are some rules of thumb:

- Morning edition papers – these reporters usually have deadlines late in the afternoon. You do not want to call and ask someone what they thought of your idea when they are on deadline. The response will likely not be warm and fuzzy.
- Weekly papers – usually have longer lead times. Ask what their deadline is upfront and be mindful of it when calling in the future.
- TV – on air personalities are hard to get in touch with. I would aim for making contact with the assignment editor or producer of a certain show. Morning show producers are hard to reach because they come in dreadfully early and usually leave by noon. Aim to call them about an hour after the show. Be prepared to leave a message and wait for a call back or email if they are interested. Don't be so persistent that you turn them off.

Timing is also important when it comes to trends. If you are providing commentary on a subject or trend, then do it within a tight timeframe of when that trend is out. Let's go back to our new cell phone scenario. Say Apple issues their new phone. You can't provide commentary on it two months after it is out there – well you can, but no one may listen or care. Be prepared to respond quickly if there is something you can be an expert on. And, if you do a good job on the first go around, the media will come back to you time and time again.

The End Result/Final Thoughts

At the end of the day stay focused on what you want the end result to be – getting free coverage of your business or idea. The important thing to remember is the steps above are a process. You just can't try it once and be done with it. Establishing a relationship with the media takes time. If you can get your foot in the door just that first time, and do a good job, then chances are withy will call you back. Repeatedly. And, while the media landscape is changing, traditional media is still out there – and they are looking for ideas. If you can be a catalyst for them, they will remember you.

About the Author:

While I'm more comfortable promoting other people, here is a little intel on me. I have a degree in broadcast and film communications from the University of Alabama. I'm also currently in the Information Engineering and Management Masters program at the University of Alabama at Birmingham (anticipated graduation date May  2013). I've worked in and around communications since college. My media experience includes everything from being an on air radio news talent to writing the evening and morning news as a television producer. I've worked for universities as well as private and publicly traded companies and one non-profit. I've been in the midst of and worked through some of the biggest crisis situations in the region including the HealthSouth financial scandal, the bombing of the New Women All Women Health Clinic near UAB, and two bank mergers. My specialties include web content, video production, crisis communication, media relations, social media management and writing for internal and external publications. In 2000, I earned national accreditation in public relations (APR) through the Public Relations Society of America (kind of like a CPA for PR people).

www.ingramcontent.com/pod-product-compliance
Lightning Source LLC
Chambersburg PA
CBHW021936170526
45157CB00005B/2331